Responding to Strategic and Organizational Uncertainty: Developing Army Leaders "after Iraq and Afghanistan"

Developing leaders is one the most important endeavors within the Army profession. Developing the right leader competencies is vital to establishing the core of "expert knowledge" essential to winning wars and defines the Army as profession. Developing leaders responsive to challenges to national security also requires an understanding of the strategic environment to prepare for the dynamic present and invest in an uncertain future. In addition to ensuring today's leaders are competent in tactical and operational levels of warfare, the profession must ensure accomplished leaders achieve their full potential as future strategic leaders. While serving as the U.S. Army Chief of Staff, General Martin E. Dempsey reinforced the importance of the Army as a "learning organization" and offered, "leader development is our true competitive advantage."[1] Yet the Army has not fully adapted its leader development programs to account for the changes in the strategic environment.

As the United States withdraws from the wars in Iraq and Afghanistan and changes its approach to the war against Al Qaeda, the U.S. Army must ensure a strategic approach to developing leaders capable of operating in this increasingly uncertain, dynamic, and volatile international security environment. The contemporary security environment reflects the influence of unconventional threats (for example, incapable or failing states, transnational terrorism and criminal organizations, cyber-war, WMD proliferation), accounts for a changing global political landscape associated with international security ("Arab Awakening," emerging powers), and includes threats to the global commons and international commerce.[2] Today's Army leaders constitute the

1

most "combat-experienced force" fielded in recent memory; however, much of this experience reflects a decade of experience in counterinsurgency that may be only partially relevant for these other strategic challenges. The 2012 Army Strategic Planning Guidance acknowledges this situation and directs the Army to "transform itself from a force that focuses on counterinsurgency operations to an Army that is operationally adaptable," and "focus on fulfilling a broader range of missions."[3] This transformation is extremely difficult in the context of strategic uncertainty.

The Army, however, faces equally important uncertainty from a second source, emerging from within its own organization. This "organizational uncertainty" surfaces from a lack of uniformity in operational experience, varied educational and technical backgrounds, anxiety about and imperfect knowledge of the security environment, and inconsistent commitment to organizational goals. Unpredictable social factors including complex interpersonal relations, varying methods of learning and sharing information among generations, and incompatible behavioral styles within the organization also add to organizational uncertainty.[4] Furthermore, limited comprehension of the intersection of these social and organizational factors complicates decision-making processes, only contributing further to uncertainty within the organization.[5] Following more than a decade of sustained conflict, organizational uncertainty manifests itself visibly in the form of suicides, traumatic brain injury (TBI), post-traumatic stress disorder (PTSD), and other health concerns.[6] In addition, differing perspectives among generations of Army officers potentially constitute antagonistic social perceptions and discontent about the Army's priorities. Lastly, recent examination of the force following a decade of war reveals an imbalance in attention to the institutional, organizational, and self-development domains of leader development, that is, the Army's three dimensions on which its leader development is built. This imbalance is not only contrary to Army doctrine, but also contributes further to organizational uncertainty.

This combination of strategic and organizational uncertainty confronts leader development efforts and reduces the Army's "competitive advantage." In the context of these external and internal complex challenges, this paper recommends options within the existing leader development model to respond to strategic and organizational uncertainty. The first section of this paper draws upon the national intelligence estimate and the U.S. Army's strategic assessment of the "world we live in" to communicate the uncertain nature of the contemporary security environment. The second section of the paper describes organizational challenges internal to the Army that, in some respects, present the more pressing challenge. This section scrutinizes sources of organizational uncertainty including differing generational perspectives, imbalance in leader development efforts, and issues of resilience that may limit otherwise fully capable tactical leaders from achieving strategic leadership potential. The third section of the paper articulates the relationship between strategic leadership competencies and these external and internal challenges confronting the U.S. Army.

In addition to reinforcing critical thinking and problem skills as components of leader development, this analysis introduces three additional competencies, "bi-lateral mentorship," accrual of personal knowledge, and "mind fitness," as essential both to developing strategic leadership competencies and mitigating factors of organizational uncertainty. These additional strategic leadership competencies cultivated over the course of a career better prepare leaders to respond to strategic uncertainty. This

3

analysis suggests "bi-lateral mentorship," accrual of personal knowledge through self-study, and "mind fitness" all offer opportunities to specifically reduce these sources of organizational uncertainty. More specifically, this report offers the following recommendations within U.S. Army strategic leader development to respond to organizational and strategic uncertainty:

1. Conduct a formal Army study examining the officer corps to confirm whether generational differences contribute to organizational uncertainty and limit leader development. Encourage bi-lateral mentorship as an opportunity for improved intergenerational communication.

2. Include more accountability in the self-development domain without losing the importance of "self" direction.

3. Introduce "Mind Fitness" training into institutional leader development programs as a critical skills-based approach to augment existing resilience programs.

Ultimately, the latter two recommendations recognize the value of self-development in reducing harmful factors of organizational uncertainty. Combined with operational and institutional opportunities that already reinforce critical thinking and problem solving skills, internalizing these self-development efforts will increase intellectual capacity, leverage practical, emotional, and social intelligence, increase attention and awareness, and invest in the long-term development of leaders better prepared for the uncertain strategic horizon.

I. External Challenge to Developing Leaders: The Uncertain Security Environment

> *I promise that the future security environment will never play out exactly the way we've envisioned.*
> — *General Martin E. Dempsey*[7]

Uncertainty and variety combine to imperil U.S. national interests and international stability. Today's security threats do not manifest themselves as a single strategic adversary.[8] As strategists, analysts, scholars, and students attempt to conceptualize the contemporary security environment, the discourse tends to acknowledge "uncertainty" as the dominant factor of the world around us. The dynamic and unpredictable combinations of possible scenarios and environments complicate the U.S. Army's "Train as you will fight" imperative central to leader development.

Contemporary scholars debate the concept of "security," and it is widely accepted that the paradigm of international security traditionally defined by relations between states is inadequate. The end of the Cold War, which was once thought to bring increased possibilities of peace and stability, instead "exposed and accelerated transnational forces that challenge traditional ideas about power and security."[9] Scholars now describe the concept of security as "broadening, stretching, or extending" to account for the inclusion of societies and individuals in the security agenda once reserved only for nation states.[10] Where the traditional paradigm primarily regarded security in terms of threat of military action within a system of nation-states, the new and broader paradigm emerged following the end of the Cold War. The attacks against the United States on September 11th, 2001 served as a watershed event to raise awareness of a security environment that includes transnational terrorism, piracy, cyber activities, refugees and displaced persons, failed or failing states, bioterrorism, nuclear proliferation, transnational terrorist and criminal enterprises, youth bulges and demography, spread of infectious diseases, ethnic rebellions, oil shortages, and the collapse of global markets.

The National Intelligence Council's (NIC) *Global Trends 2030: Alternative Worlds* attempts to provide a long-term strategic estimate of the uncertain future and routinely serves as a source document in strategic U.S. policy decisions. Mathew Burroughs, principal author of the report, warned that while each of the "relative uncertainties" (possible future scenarios) presents inherent complexities, the wide "breadth" in range of these possible "uncertain futures" is even more alarming. He further cautioned this variation between "plausible worst case" and "plausible best case" scenarios will likely widen, and the nature of unpredictable events such as climate change poses even more significant implications with respect to security.[11] In exploring this range of "malleable futures," the NIC's *Global Trends 2030* constructs a relationship among megatrends, game-changers, "Black Swans," and human agency to provide a framework of possible future scenarios (see Figure 1). Megatrends that exist today, and are likely to gain momentum, include empowerment of individuals accounting for the expansion of the global middle class, access to communications technologies, and advances in manufacturing and health-care; diffusion of power describing the shift from hegemonic powers to a multipolar world, changes in demography from aging populations, youth bulges, and urbanization; and the growing demand for food, water, and energy resources resulting from population growth.[12]

Strategic uncertainty encompasses possible future scenarios ranging from "Stalled Engines" following a halt in globalization and U.S. retrenchment, to "Fusion" resulting from unanticipated global cooperation, possibly including collaboration between the U.S. and China. Other possibilities include the uncontrollable "Gini Out of the Bottle" unleashed from increasing social inequalities, failed states, and lack of U.S. intervention; or a "Non-state World" where non-state actors capitalize on their technological advantages to assume the lead role in tackling global challenges.[13] The NIC report further highlights, "extrapolations of the megatrends would alone point to a changed world by 2030 – but the world could be transformed in radically different ways."[14] The influence of human agency in the form of "critical game changers" or the emergence of "Black Swans" (highly improbable events that are unpredictable and have a massive impact)[15] below will ultimately determine the global environment in future decades.[16]

This framework of "Alternative worlds," entirely representative of strategic uncertainty, presents enormous difficulties in replicating scenarios for training and leader development. The recently published *U.S. Army Capstone Concept* describes the Army's responsibilities in support of U.S. strategic objectives and acknowledges, "The uncertainty and complexity of the future operational environment will require the Army to respond to a broad range of threats and challenges."[18] Unlike the circumstances following the Vietnam War where the Army largely expunged counterinsurgency skills to return to the possibility of conventional war in Europe,[19] today's U.S. Army must retain the vast array of skills associated with recent operations while also preparing for a diverse range of contingencies that span the globe (Figure 2). Furthermore, to respond to strategic uncertainty the U.S. Army in the 21st century must develop leaders capable of supporting land component forces with an expanding range of complex missions including: conducting counterterrorism and irregular warfare, detering and defeat aggression, projecting power despite anti-access and area denial challenges, countering weapons of mass destruction (WMD), operating effectively in space, operating effectively in cyberspace, maintaining a nuclear deterrent, defending the homeland and provide Defense Support of Civil Authorities (DSCA), providing a stabilizing presence, conducting stability and counterinsurgency operations, and conducting humanitarian, disaster relief, and other operations.[20]

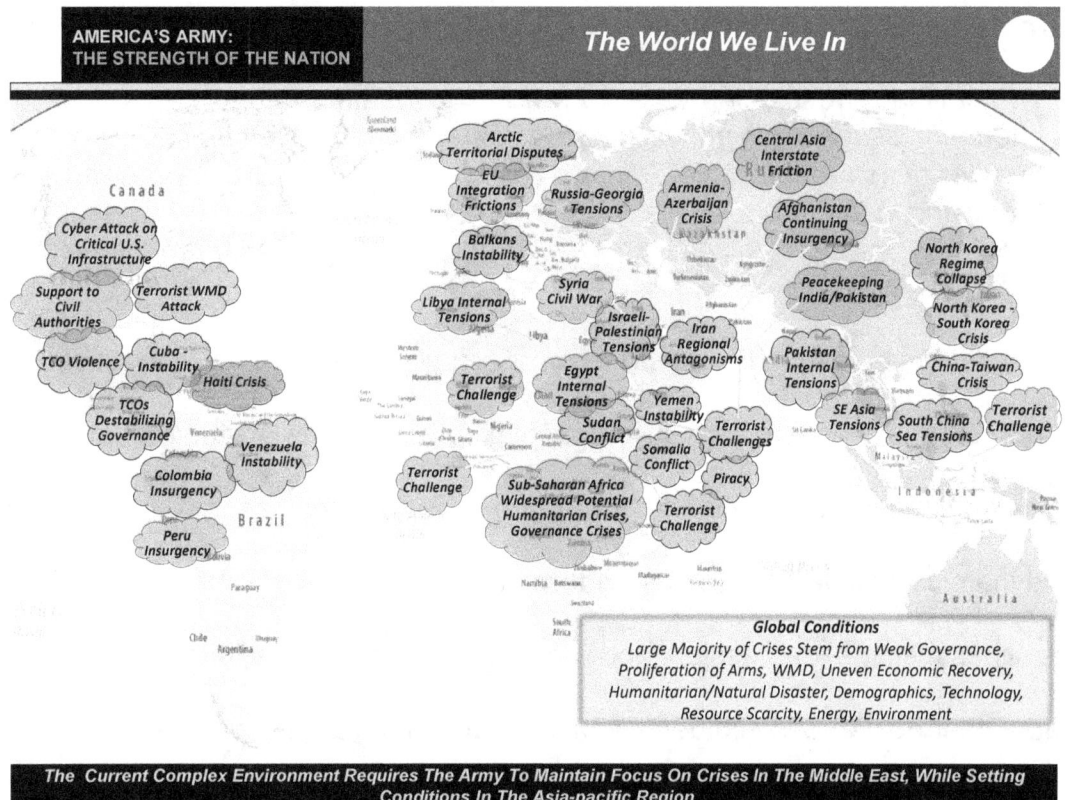

Global Conditions
Large Majority of Crises Stem from Weak Governance, Proliferation of Arms, WMD, Uneven Economic Recovery, Humanitarian/Natural Disaster, Demographics, Technology, Resource Scarcity, Energy, Environment

The Current Complex Environment Requires The Army To Maintain Focus On Crises In The Middle East, While Setting Conditions In The Asia-pacific Region

Figure 2: "The World We Live In", U.S. Army Vision[21]

While responding to uncertainty is not new to the U.S. Army, the range of uncertain scenarios in the 21st century presents increased complexity and volatility. Time is also a factor. The "flash to bang" time in the hyper-connected, instant media world adds pressure to decision-making and response.[22] As the U.S. Army prepares for the next battle, an examination of "first battles" following previous strategic transitions reveal that as war increases in complexity, emphasis on creative leadership, above all other factors, "simplifies the complexities of war and thus renders the combat environment more manageable."[23] The uncertain and unpredictable future reinforces the importance of developing leaders capable of internalizing strategic leadership competencies necessary to preserve a competitive advantage and to succeed in combat operations and other missions.

II. Internal Challenges to Developing Leaders: People as a Source of Uncertainty

> *The obvious stress of ten years of war in two theaters and myriad attendant issues like high suicide rates, stress on Families and a rising number of non-deployable Soldiers have real implications for the Army today and in the future.*
>
> — *John M. McHugh, Secretary of the Army[24]*

In addition to responding to strategic uncertainty, the U.S. Army must similarly respond to organizational uncertainty. Complex, pressing and unstable human dynamics originating from within the profession adversely limit leader development. These dynamics include the obvious and well-documented effects of war manifesting in injuries, illness, stress, depression, and other issues that linger after soldiers return from combat. Other destabilizing influences include differing perspectives between generations of officers and an imbalance in leader development.

The Army recognizes aspects of organizational uncertainty and is attempting to deal with them; however, sources of organizational uncertainty intersect and are deeply embedded in the profession following more than a decade of conflict. Competing generational perspectives present different opinions as to how to address organizational uncertainty, and also result in different perspectives about strategic leadership potential. Additionally, success in spite of an imbalance in leader development not only reinforces bad habits, but also allows leaders to progress to their next rank lacking some of the training, experience, and educational attributes necessary to succeed. During a period of strategic transition following wars in Iraq and Afghanistan, these sources of organizational uncertainty are potentially more dangerous for the U.S. Army than the strategic uncertainty described in the previous section. In examining organizational uncertainty, this analysis refers to a specific collection of strategic leadership competencies emerging from a U.S. Army War College's Strategic Studies Institute (SSI) study to illustrate the relationship between organizational uncertainties and strategic leadership potential. The 2003 SSI analysis identified strategic leadership "metacompetencies" from their examination of both Army Training and Leader Development Panel reports and popular literature on strategic leadership. These "metacompetencies" include identity, mental agility, cross-cultural savvy, interpersonal maturity, "World Class Warrior" (referred to as strategic military expertise), and professional astuteness.[25] Figure 3 (below) describes the characteristics of each of these "metacompetencies."

Strategic Leadership "Metacompetency"	Characteristics
Identity	*Identity* is self-awareness and maturity that includes understanding of one's values and how they integrate with the Army values.[26]
Mental Agility	*Mental Agility* stresses adaptability, decision-making skills, improvisation, "cognitive complexity," and the ability to scan and adjust learning based on the environment.[27]
Cross-Cultural Savvy	*Cross-cultural savvy* demonstrates the ability to understand a culture beyond one's organizational, economic, religious, societal, geographical, and political boundaries.[28]
Interpersonal Maturity	*Interpersonal Maturity* demonstrates an understanding of strategic relationships, and the ability to "analyze, challenge, and change and organization's culture to align it with the ever changing outside environment."[29]
Strategic Military Expertise (Referred to as the "World Class Warrior")	*Strategic Military Expertise* includes understanding of the entire spectrum of operations at the strategic level, such as theater strategy, campaign strategy, joint, interagency, and multinational operations, and the ability to use the elements of national power and technology to execute national security strategy.[30]
Professional Astuteness	*Professional Astuteness* demonstrates the insight to do what is best for the profession and the nation. This includes political savvy, recognizing when to compromise, understanding the Army serves multiple constituencies, and ensuring the officer corps maintains its expertise in national defense while adhering to a professional ethic.[31]

Figure 3: Strategic Leadership "Metacompetencies"[32]

The breadth of possible scenarios requires cultivation of all of these strategic leadership metacompetencies to develop leaders capable of responding to this uncertainty. However, three principal sources of organizational uncertainty counter and degrade these strategic leadership competencies, as illustrated on the right side of Figure 4 below. The sections that follow illustrate how generational rifts negatively influence identity, cross-cultural savvy, interpersonal maturity, and professional astuteness. Similarly, imbalance in leader development efforts limits potential in all of the six strategic leadership metacompetencies. Lastly, issues of undermined resilience and fatigue negatively influence leader's identity, mental agility, cross-cultural savvy and strategic military expertise. The resulting degradation in strategic leadership competencies ultimately limits the organization's capacity to respond to strategic uncertainty.

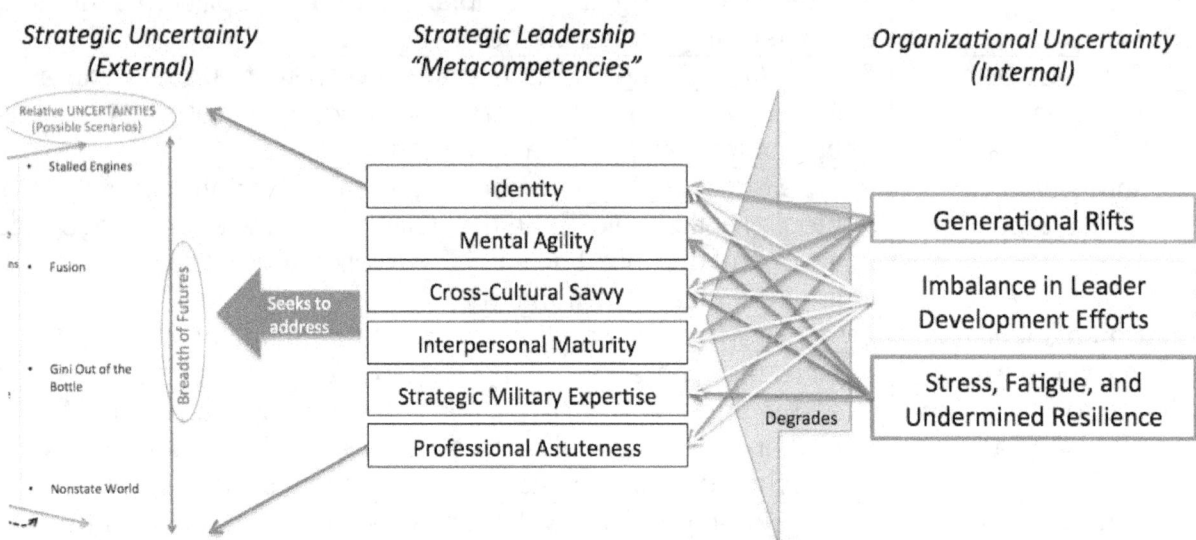

Figure 4: Relationship between Strategic Uncertainty, Organizational Uncertainty, and Strategic Leadership "Metacompetencies"

Source of Organizational Uncertainty #1: Differences in Generational Perspectives

Differing perspectives among generations of officers within the profession contributes to organizational uncertainty. As the nation and the U.S. Army conduct the strategic transition following more than a decade of war, cohorts of officers from different generations possess remarkably different opinions about the future opportunities and challenges facing the profession. The issues presented by differing generational perspectives are not new to the U.S. Army, and in fact, are often typical among hierarchical organizations possessing a wide range of age and experience within their ranks. However, generational rifts following the wars in Iraq and Afghanistan contribute to organizational uncertainty and degrade strategic leadership competencies.

Today's officer corps hosts three separate but related generations of officers: those commissioned or recruited since 2001, who only know an Army at war ("post 9/11" officers); senior leaders whose tactical experience was primarily defined by the post-Vietnam and Cold War Army ("Cold War" officers); and those in between (referred to as "hybrid" officers given tactical level experience in Iraq, Afghanistan and in Cold War training environments).[33] Previous examinations of differing generational perceptions reveal these differences contribute to organizational uncertainty. For example, about a decade ago, differences between two generations of officers led to an alarming exodus of junior officers and triggered an Army-wide Blue Ribbon Panel to examine the root cause and attempt to reverse the trend. Examining this recent incident offers insight into how the existence of three generations today further fuels organizational uncertainty.

Before the wars in Iraq and Afghanistan, another SSI sponsored study, "Generations Apart: Xers and Boomers in the Officer Corps," concluded that a lack understanding of generational perspectives not only frustrated junior officers, but also jeopardized readiness and future leadership of the Army. Beyond the impact of higher attrition rates on the organization, the younger generation's increased capacity for discussion and interaction using electronic means also allowed wider dissemination of discontent, a result not conducive to organizational goals. This discussion often "resulted in debilitating conflict within the Army."[34] Dr. Leonard Wong's report identified the source of conflict emerging from two distinct generations of officers defined by either the Baby Boom Generation (born between 1943 and 1960) or Generation X (born between 1960 and 1980). Today, the "Boomers" constitute senior leaders with tactical experience largely defined by the post-Vietnam and Cold War Army (Cold War officers), and "Xers" refer to "hybrid" officers possessing tactical level experience in Iraq, Afghanistan and in Cold War training environments.

Dr. Wong pointed out, "Generational differences emerge as cohorts experience defining moments in history which shape their attitudes and perspectives."[35] Without the benefit of hindsight following 11 years of war, Wong's monograph predicted in 2000, "the newly minted second lieutenants that enter the Army this year are not Generation X...instead they are Generation Y, the Nintendo Generation, Generation 2001, or Generation Next."[36] This generation of officers commissioned after 2001 largely define themselves by their tactical experience in Iraq and Afghanistan. This generation also experienced the rapid proliferation of smartphones and expansion of social media as a means to communicate with an even greater range of communications methodologies

14

and learning opportunities. Lastly, as commissioned officers, this generation only understands life in an "Army at war" following the attacks on September 11, 2001.

A more recent 2010 U.S. Army War College report reviewing leadership behaviors and organizational climates within Army Divisions also observed harmful differences between generations. While the subject of generations was not the focus of the report, the author noted that the subject warranted attention.[37] Of 72 Captains interviewed as part of the 2010 study, the majority of whom deployed at least twice, the respondents viewed "a considerable percentage of officers at higher than Brigade Combat Team (BCT) levels as 'out of touch.'"[38] Officers surveyed also tended to view the constraints imposed while at home station as trivial, distrustful, and counter to the latitude they enjoyed while deployed. The study suggested that the "gap" in expectations between the deployed and garrison environments "represents a significant institutional issue."[39] This generational dissatisfaction contributes to organizational uncertainty.

Although there are no recent Army studies specifically examining generational perspectives, interviews of forty officers, from captain to general on the subject of leader development conducted for this paper, confirmed the troubling observations from the previous studies. While anecdotal, the response from these officers potentially indicates continued divisions among generations and creates concerns about organizational uncertainty. To preserve a level of methodological credibility, the sample population interviewed included officers committed to service in the profession, not potentially disgruntled officers considering separation from the Army. In this sample, captains and majors included graduate students participating in advanced civil schooling opportunities, Ranger Rifle Company commanders possessing multiple combat command tours, and current professors at the United States Military Academy. All lieutenant colonels and colonels interviewed had commanded at the battalion level. All general officers interviewed held levels of responsibility appropriate to their rank.

It is difficult to generalize from such a small sample of forty officers; however, when combined with the findings from previous examinations of how generational differences influence organizational uncertainty, there are a number of relevant parallels. Of thirty-four officers interviewed, ranging from captain to colonel, all but three interviewees believed the Army currently consists of three separate but related generations of leaders as described at the beginning of this section. Among a sample of six active duty general officers, three also agreed there are three generations of officers. The remaining six officers (including three general officers) agreed that generational perspectives contribute to organizational uncertainty, but maintained that Cold War officers who failed to adapt to the operational environments in Iraq and Afghanistan are no longer in the Army today. In contrast, the younger officers interviewed did not share this perception about the departure of Cold War influences, serving as a good example of generational rifts.[40]

Further, this small sample suggested that organizational uncertainty emerges from a lack of uniformity in experience, inconsistent levels of commitment to the organization, and differing social perspectives. All of these factors appear in descriptions of generational traits. The twenty-four officers commissioned after 2001 ("post 9/11" generation) generally prided themselves on their tactical competency, innovation, independence, cultural sensitivity, and idealism. They also confessed to a

16

lack of humility, a sense of entitlement gained from enduring the hardship of multiple deployments in assignments at the company level and below, a tendency to discount experience of officers senior to them, and a lack of experience in training management. They recognized senior officers as proficient planners, expert trainers skilled in conventional warfare, and leaders with diverse responsibilities. However, these young officers were suspicious of the older officers' (pre 9/11 officers) tendencies to micromanage subordinates, inflexibility, careerism, emphasis on metrics and "measures of effectiveness" not related to tactical effects, and lack of consistency in tactical combat experience.[41]

In contrast, the sixteen officers commissioned prior to 2001 considered their operational experience they gained in Desert Storm, Bosnia, Kosovo, Macedonia, and Somalia as essential to meeting the challenges in Iraq and Afghanistan. They also valued their knowledge of doctrine and understanding of larger systems that contribute to the effectiveness of the profession. These officers acknowledged the tactical experience, energy, creativity, ability to adapt to new technologies, and social connectivity of the "post-9/11" generation. However, they also shared concerns about younger officers' lack of experience in training management resulting from prescriptive Army Force Generation cycles (ARFORGEN), over-reliance on applying a narrow base of experience to solve all problems, lack of discipline, tendency to accept mediocre work as the norm, lack of familiarity in combined arms maneuver, and lack of tolerance (bordering on disrespect) of hierarchy and bureaucracy. They also confided that officers commissioned after 2001 fail to recognize that the Army will not, and should not, remain in a perpetual state of war.[42]

Lastly, the sample population of both "post-9/11" and hybrid officers perceive that Cold War officers possess a wealth of experience, understand that military campaigns require clearly defined objectives, and offer valuable strategic perspective and maturity to the profession. However, "post 9/11" and hybrid officers also view the Cold War generation as inflexible "linear-fighters" who are slow to accept tactical realities from the "bottom up." They feel that Cold War officers often focus on tactical problems and miss the strategic problems requiring their attention.[43]

These broad overviews of generational attributes highlight significant factors of organizational uncertainty and obstacles to achieving strategic leadership competencies. Admissions of arrogance and a lack of humility among "post-9/11" officers clearly interfere with "Identity" and integration of one's values with the Army values. Habits of micromanagement and inflexibility among the two senior generations is contrary to embracing empowerment as an attribute necessary for "Interpersonal Maturity" and jeopardize the development of subordinates in fully achieving the same. Furthermore, reliance on a narrow base of experience and lack of familiarity in combined arms maneuver limit young officers from achieving strategic military expertise and becoming "world class warriors." Lastly, all officers subscribing to narrow generational perspectives may dismiss strategic guidance from current senior Army leaders that is inconsistent with their personal observations and experience, resulting in a "loss in translation" of important strategic intent. In the long-term, narrow generational perspectives limit the potential of capable officers in recognizing their potential as strategic leaders.

Source of Organizational Uncertainty #2: Imbalance in Army Leader Development

Imbalance in Army leader development efforts also serves as a source of organizational uncertainty. The Army leader development model (figure 5) is based on the relationship among the three mutually supporting domains of learning that contribute to developing leadership skills and attributes progressively throughout an Army career. These domains include the operational, institutional, and self-development domains, all of which prepare leaders for assuming additional responsibility.

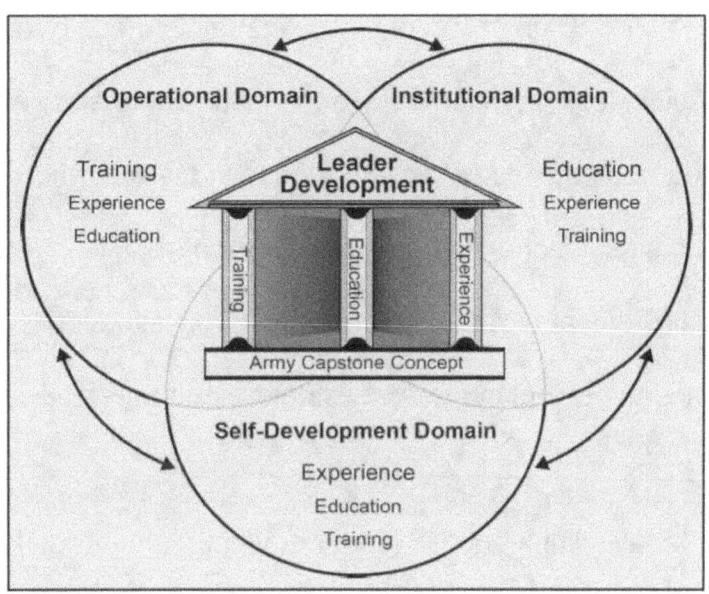

Figure 5: Army Leader Development Model[44]

The operational domain includes experience gained during contingency operations, training activities at home station, rotations at a Combat Training Center (CTC), or unit level leader professional development sessions (LPDs). The institutional domain accounts for attendance at schools and professional military education (PME) to obtain knowledge, skills, and practice necessary to perform critical tasks. The self-development domain is an individual responsibility and consists of independent study to enhance learning in the operational and institutional domain, address gaps in skills and knowledge, or prepare for future responsibilities.[45] In addition, the self-development domain includes three types of self-development: structured, guided, and personal. Structured self-development is required, planned, goal-oriented learning sponsored by the institution (the Army). Guided self-development is optional learning that follows a progressive sequence with contributions from the chain of command, and personal self-development is initiated and defined by the individual.[46]

Each of these domains is necessary for effective leader development, but none is sufficient by itself. Yet the combination of time constraints, pace of operations, and personal choice result in less attention paid to the institutional and self-development domains.[47] While leaders rely heavily on experience in the operational domain, the decreased reliance on institutional and self-development results in a narrow range of expertise only partially relevant for future scenarios. This situation is not only a source of organizational uncertainty, but in the Army's next "first battle" this is also a source of great risk.

In hindsight, today's imbalance in leader development efforts is easily explained. The recent decade of conflict in Iraq and Afghanistan provided unprecedented opportunities for learning within the operational domain. In some cases, however, frequent deployments reduced opportunities within the institutional and self-development domains. Primary examples of this case include the backlog of mid-grade officers needing to attend Intermediate Level Education (ILE) and the lack of time available for self-development opportunities given the pace of operations. In the effort to address short-term challenges and keep "combat seasoned leaders in the fight," officers delayed or waived attendance at professional military schools. Ultimately, this compromised long-term benefits of progressive learning within the institutional domain.[48] PME venues also generally lag in documenting operational lessons to share within the institutional domain. The Army continues to document many of the operational lessons from Iraq and Afghanistan. General Martin Dempsey, now the Chairman of the Joint Chiefs of Staff, cautioned, "This doctrine [learned from these operations] does not pervade the force," and "until it does, we cannot consider ourselves ready, and we should not consider ourselves sufficiently adaptable for future contingencies."[49]

An imbalance in leader development degrades all six of the strategic leadership metacompetencies. Lack of commitment to self-development combined with an over-reliance on operational experience limit self-awareness necessary to achieve "identity." Mental agility similarly requires a diverse foundation of knowledge learned in all three domains of leader development to adapt, recognize changes in environments, improvise, and achieve an appropriate level of "cognitive complexity." Lack of exploration beyond operational experience also limits cross-cultural savvy and interpersonal maturity, as both require knowledge that extends beyond boundaries of personal experience and environment. An imbalance in leader development, particularly where leaders reduce attention to the institutional domain, limits understanding the entire spectrum of national strategy and joint, combined, interagency and multinational operations necessary to achieve strategic military expertise. Lastly, failure to dedicate time and attention to all three domains of leader development is contrary to Army doctrine and inconsistent with the Army's professional ethic. Professionally astute leaders cannot ensure or advance this ethic within the officer corps if they cannot comply with it themselves.

Source of Organizational Uncertainty #3: Lack of Resilience and Fatigue following War

Issues of resilience and fatigue directly resulting from prolonged combat serve as a third source of organizational uncertainty. On January 14, 2013, the Associated Press released a sobering statistic that captured national attention and portrayed a dire organizational trend. Department of Defense suicide data disclosed the "number of active-duty suicides in 2012 reached an all-time record – with the 349 self-inflicted deaths far exceeding American combat deaths during the same period."[50] The suicide rate among Army personnel is merely one indicator of the level of stress and fatigue on the force following more than a decade of war. The long-term effects of a prolonged period of war given unpredictable long-term psychological and physiological effects on the capability of the force constitute one of the Army's greatest organizational uncertainties. Adding to the uncertainty, it is also impossible to predict when harmful psychological and physiological effects will manifest among afflicted Soldiers and leaders.

The Department of the Army recently published *Army 2020: Generating Health & Discipline in the Force Ahead of the Strategic Reset* (commonly referred to as *The Army Gold Book*) to inform and educate leaders regarding the challenges facing the Army in terms of combat related wounds, injuries, and illnesses including TBI, PTSD, depression, stress, and suicide. The following statistics illustrate this challenge:

- U.S. Army 2010 research statistics reflect that approximately 20% of more than two million Service members who deployed will develop PTSD.[51]

- Veterans Administration health records reflect that depression affects approximately 32% of Soldiers. Depression commonly leads to substance abuse in an attempt to cope with symptoms.[52]

- The 2011 U.S. Army Posture Statement revealed that "roughly 47%" of Soldiers returning from deployment report pain-related health concerns resulting in increased prescription of pharmaceuticals. Fourteen percent of Soldiers received "opioid painkillers with oxycodone" and 23-25% of wounded Soldiers are addicted to prescription or illegal drugs while awaiting medical discharge.[53]

- A 2008 U.S. Army study revealed 30% of deployed Soldiers suffered from difficulty sleeping (58% of Soldiers with head injuries reported sleep problems). In addition, 8% of deployed Soldiers routinely relied on mental health medications to overcome difficulty sleeping.[54] The *Army Gold Book* reported that sleep disturbances are common among redeployed veterans and many Soldiers who have difficulty sleeping resort to "self-medication" using alcohol or drugs only further reducing their performance.[55]

While the *Army Gold Book* seeks to inform and educate leaders, the statistics account for detrimental conditions present in leaders themselves. In addition to hardship in battle, the weight of leadership responsibilities and the associated stress similarly contribute to post-traumatic symptoms. Leaders often attempt to cope without assistance or mask symptoms, resulting in avoidance or emotional detachment, difficulty sleeping, and issues with concentration and memory.[56] An examination of PTSD among the Command and General Staff College Class of 2008 revealed almost 40% of 297 field grade officers surveyed presented symptoms of PTSD. Well over half of the surveyed officers also believed that seeking mental health counseling would harm their careers.[57] Five years later, these officers are now approaching zones of consideration for battalion command.

The U.S. Army acknowledges that the complexity of identifying and diagnosing the population of Soldiers suffering from TBI, PTSD, or anxiety related illnesses "may play out as the *most significant challenge confronting the Army's human domain and force readiness* as the Army transitions from war (emphasis added)."[58] This aspect of organizational uncertainty also clearly degrades the strategic leadership metacompetencies of identity, mental agility, and strategic military expertise. Soldiers suffering from fatigue and sleep disturbances, particularly those who compensate with extensive use of medication, often display some measure of cognitive impairment, which limits self-awareness and adaptability critical for decision-making skills. Similarly, leaders may avoid training scenarios that replicate traumatic combat experiences, thereby reducing the quality of the training events and also limiting the potential to gain strategic expertise. The Army continues to improve methods for preventing and treating across the range of combat related injuries and illnesses. While this is necessary, it is not sufficient.[59]

As this section has demonstrated, these issues today can increase organizational uncertainty and degrade leader metacompetencies. However, the following section will elaborate on specific measures to mitigate the harmful influences of generational rifts, the imbalance in leader development, and the lack of resilience resulting from fatigue and stress, while also reinforcing and developing strategic leadership competencies.

III. Responding to Strategic (External) and Organizational (Internal) Uncertainty

We must adapt our ability to develop our leaders for the future...it is imperative that we properly develop them to think through these complex problems, operate in these complex environments and uncertain situations they will surely experience.
— *General Raymond Odierno, U.S. Army Chief of Staff*[60]

The previous sections outlined the sources of strategic and organizational uncertainty that exist today in the midst of a major strategic transition following wars in Iraq and Afghanistan. When confronted by uncertainty and unpredictability, all leaders, and especially strategic leaders, need to comprehend the external and internal sources of uncertainty.[61] Lessons from previous post-conflict transitions reinforce the essential role of leader development arguing that "the competence and character of individual leaders at all levels, uniformed and civilian, is the single most influential factor in the Army being, and remaining, a military profession."[62]

While the Army deliberately seeks to address strategic uncertainty through progressive cultivation of strategic leadership competencies, the Army has not focused sufficiently on organizational uncertainty or its effects. Nor has the Army sufficiently examined the intersection of both strategic uncertainty and organizational uncertainty. Leader development efforts designed to reinforce and develop strategic leadership competencies are necessary but insufficient. Leader development efforts must also deliberately address factors of organizational uncertainty, and the way these factors intersect with strategic uncertainty. This report suggests leader development efforts reinforce critical thinking and problem solving skills with "bi-lateral mentorship," accrual of personal knowledge, and "mind fitness" to respond to strategic and organizational uncertainty.

Critical thinking and problem solving remain fundamental components of the U.S. Army's leader development process for responding to strategic uncertainty and developing strategic leadership competencies. The Army continues to evolve methods to nurture these first two talents throughout an officer's career. Even prior to commissioning, the United States Military Academy (USMA) reinforces critical thinking and problem solving skills essential to future leaders through "Project Based Education and Research" and scientific evaluation. These instructional methods allow students to test assumptions and develop hypotheses and avoid reliance on short-term memorization from the discarded "Thayer Method," which emphasized homework and student presentations.[63]

From within the operational domain, expanding scenarios beyond Iraq and Afghanistan at the Combat Training Centers (CTCs), and exploring Outcomes Based Training and Education (OBT&E) offer additional opportunities to exercise critical thinking and problem-solving skills, and develop adaptive leaders. Aligning with the Army Force Generation Model (ARFORGEN) to meet operational requirements in Iraq and Afghanistan necessitated a narrow focus on rehearsal of "known" missions. However, according to General Robert Cone, Commanding General of Training and Doctrine Command (TRADOC), this occurred to "the detriment of broader thinking" among leaders.[64] Today, the "Decisive Action Training Environment" (DATE) employs current intelligence to create realistic environments and conditions that Army units are likely to encounter.[65] These training advancements at the CTCs not only develop leadership competencies, but also provide venues to correct deficiencies resulting from narrowly focused training for a generation of officers. "Winning" as a measure of success at the CTCs should not become the focus of the leader development experience. Rather, emphasis on critical thinking and problem solving within a wide range of unfamiliar scenarios must remain central to the CTC experience. Recognizing that traditional training environments will likely not meet all future needs, retired Major Donald Vandergriff of the Asymmetric Warfare Group introduced "Adaptive Leaders Methodology (ALM)" within the OBT&E initiative to encourage critical thinking and problem solving within a learning organization. ALM discourages the "assembly line mentality" of competency-based training and instead emphasizes situational decision-making that requires leaders to find answers for themselves, resulting in refinement of their intuition and promoting adaptability.[66]

While essential to strategic leader development, critical thinking and problem solving skills do not directly address the three sources of organizational uncertainty discussed in this analysis. Thus, to counter these issues of organizational uncertainty during a period of strategic transition, this report introduces "bi-lateral mentorship," accrual of personal knowledge, and "mind fitness" as possible solutions within the self-development domain of the Army leader development model.

Bi-lateral mentorship is a reciprocal relationship where both the senior and junior officer are actively involved and mutually benefit from each other's mentorship. Today, bilateral mentorship acknowledges the tactical experience of junior officers and the operational and strategic experience of senior officers following the wars in Iraq and Afghanistan, and it encourages mutual intergenerational communication to share military expertise and help both groups become more professionally astute. An emphasis on the accrual of personal knowledge[67] results in obvious gains of explicit knowledge and offers wider contextual understanding for better employing tacit knowledge.[68] This expanded base of knowledge provides additional "know-how" to make effective decisions; it also improves mental agility and interpersonal maturity through increased understanding of environments and situations. Mind fitness offers tangible benefits for strategic leader development by training leaders to employ a wider range of coping skills in stressful environments, increasing attention skills and cognitive flexibility, and improving emotional and social intelligence.[69] The attributes gained through mind fitness offset harmful manifestations of stress and fatigue, and directly enhance the strategic leadership competencies of identity, mental agility, cross-cultural savvy, and strategic military expertise.

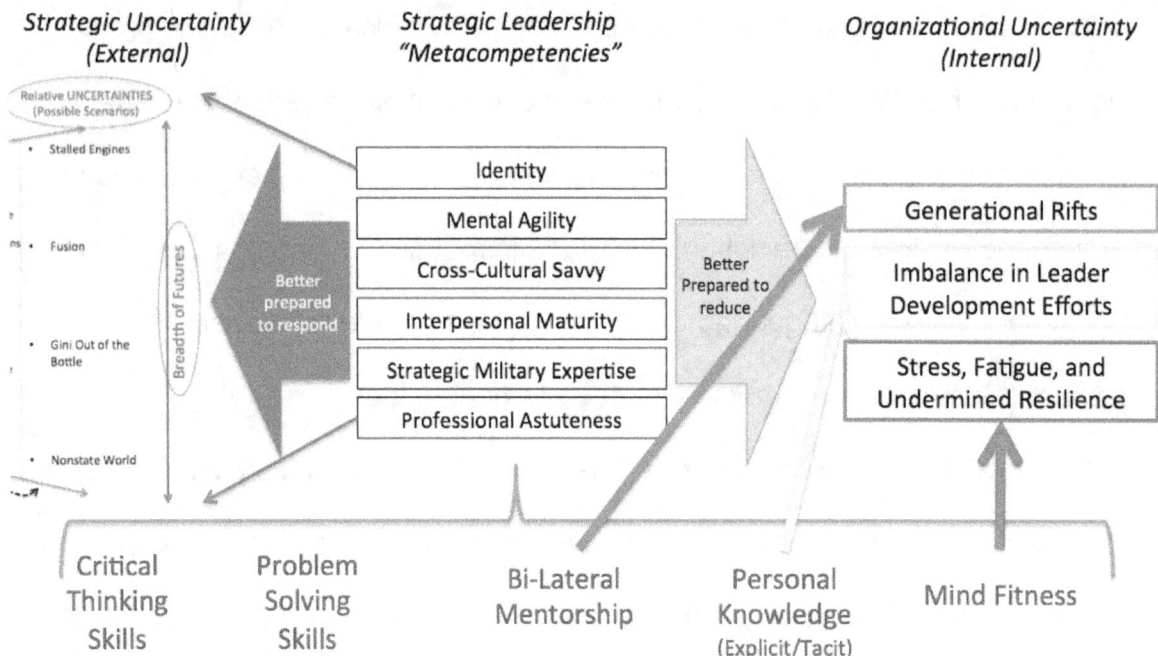

Figure 6: Components of Contemporary Leader Development

Figure 6 illustrates the relationship among bi-lateral mentorship, personal knowledge, and mind fitness in counteracting the detrimental effects of organizational uncertainty. These three components also enhance the capacity to respond to strategic

28

uncertainty and provide leaders with the tools to recognize and deal with organizational uncertainty. The following section elaborates on specific recommendations in greater detail.

Recommendation #1: Conduct a formal U.S. Army study examining the officer corps to confirm whether potential differences in generational perspectives contribute to organizational uncertainty and limit leader development. Encourage bi-lateral mentorship as an opportunity for improved intergenerational communication.

Given evidence of generational rifts, a formal examination of the generations within the Army would offer the opportunity to determine how generational perspectives serve as a source of organizational uncertainty. However, during the current strategic transition, mentorship between generations of officers already serves as an extremely valuable component of leader development. Effective mentorship that emphasizes two-way intergenerational communication may potentially dispel or reduce perceived generational issues.

The U.S. Army Mentorship Handbook credits mentorship for "increasing the effectiveness of leader developmental activities and generally producing leaders who are comfortable with the responsibilities of senior level positions."[70] The handbook also defines roles and responsibilities of "mentor" and "mentee" akin to the relationship of coach and student. While acknowledging that both individuals expand their interpersonal and leadership skills through the mentorship relationship, the handbook argues that it is the mentor who passes knowledge to the mentee. In today's context of organizational uncertainty, however, bi-lateral mentorship differs from traditional mentorship by encouraging "reverse" mentorship to occur in conjunction with traditional mentorship. "Reverse mentorship" suggests bi-lateral sharing of knowledge, where both mentor and mentee draw mutual experiential benefits from each other without sacrificing the traditional expectations of senior and junior officer conduct.

Reflecting on his experience as the Commanding General of the Joint Special Operations Command, retired General Stanley McChrystal observed an "inversion of expertise" where changes among younger generations of leadership outpaced his experience. Recognizing this could lead to concerns of credibility and legitimacy, he recommended that leaders today must be more transparent and more willing to listen to their subordinates. He suggested that this "brand new style of leadership" required "reverse mentoring" from young leaders to gain credibility and build a shared sense of purpose among people of many ages and talents.[71]

The concept of "reverse mentorship" gained attention in business to leverage the energy and creativity of younger generations, reduce turnover among younger employees, and build trust.[72] Given perceived strengths and weaknesses among generations of Army officers, bi-lateral mentorship has merit in clarifying positions and perceptions and mitigating organizational uncertainty. The Army should encourage and facilitate bi-lateral mentorship while preserving the important voluntary aspect of the traditional relationship between mentor and mentee. Raising awareness of the mutual benefits of such relationships increases the intergenerational communication necessary to fully cultivate strategic leadership competencies and benefit the U.S. Army in the future.

Recommendation #2: Modify Army leader development doctrine to include more accountability in the self-development domain without losing the importance of "self" direction.

Army doctrine already directs leaders to participate in self-development, yet the statistics reveal otherwise. The 2011 Center for Army Leadership's Annual Survey of Army Leadership (CASAL) revealed that leaders, particularly company grade officers, pay less attention to the self-development domain than the other domains. In addition, all leaders surveyed maintain that education from the institutional domain is less beneficial to their development than experience gained in the operational domain.[73] In response, TRADOC continues to address issues of confidence in the institutional domain through tangible adaptations in infrastructure improvements, curriculum revisions, and manning changes. However, the self-development domain by nature lacks visible signals of change, thereby potentially contributing to decreased attention and emphasis.

Increased organizational emphasis on, and more importantly accountability within, the self-development domain would increase the foundation of knowledge among Army leaders. For those who actively pursue and encourage self-study opportunities, accountability in self-development is not revolutionary. For others not prone to habits of independent self-study, this emphasis on personal self-development could offset the organizational uncertainty resulting from an imbalance in leader development. Over the course of a career, the resulting gain in personal knowledge in a variety of subjects could supplement progressive development of all six strategic metacompetencies. This self-development concept is not new, as other professions require individuals to maintain accreditation and currency on their own (i.e., licensed engineers, surgeons).

In highlighting personal self-development, this report does not disregard the importance of the operational and institutional domains, as these domains clearly serve as a foundation in developing critical thinking and problem solving skills essential to preparing leaders and units for dynamic environments. Yet, experience, education, and training gained in the operational and institutional domains simply cannot address all possible future scenarios. The accrual of personal knowledge, whether explicit knowledge gained through study or tacit knowledge gained through personal experience, enhances the ability to implement creative solutions and mitigate uncertainty. Where increases in explicit knowledge result directly from formal instruction or traditional study, tacit knowledge "resists introspection and articulation…[and is] defined as knowledge that people do not know they have and/or find difficult to articulate."[74] Tacit knowledge is also "personal knowledge drawn from everyday experience that helps individuals solve real-world practical problems."[75] Tacit knowledge is not only a measure of practical intelligence, but it is also essential to intuition and provides more innate opportunity to adapt to and shape the environment around us.[76]

A 1998 Army Research Institute study of tacit knowledge revealed its many practical benefits. This study compared tacit knowledge inventories among a sampling of platoon leaders, company commanders, and battalion commanders and evaluated the relationship between tacit knowledge and military leadership; quantified whether tacit knowledge was an indicator of success; and assessed applicability of tacit knowledge in leader development. The study revealed that at all three echelons (platoon, company, and battalion), tacit knowledge ratings directly correlated with ratings of effectiveness among superiors, peers, and subordinates.[77] Furthermore, increased tacit knowledge among battalion commanders clearly assisted them in "communicating a vision, helping subordinates identify strengths and weaknesses, and using subordinates as change agents."[78]

Intuitively combining tacit knowledge with broader explicit knowledge gained through personal self-development improves practical intelligence and cannot help but improve the profession's ability respond to uncertainty.[79] When leaders face an uncertain and unpredictable environment, success on the battlefield places a premium on improvisation, an essential component of mental agility. Improvisation is about "making something out of previous experience and knowledge."[80] Self-development efforts that deliberately seek to explore a wide range of unfamiliar topics only broaden the foundation of explicit knowledge necessary for problem solving in uncertain, complex environments.

The significant limitation of personal self-development is that it remains an individual responsibility. As Army doctrine acknowledges, "For self-development to be effective, all Soldiers must be completely honest with themselves to understand personal strengths and gaps in knowledge…and then take the appropriate, continuing steps."[81] In reality, the 2011 CASAL survey revealed that only about two-thirds of Army leaders specifically understand what to address in support of their own self-development. This deficiency was particularly evident in the ranks of company grade officers, where only 56% of these officers understood where they should focus self-development efforts.[82] In addition, the survey reflected less time afforded to participate in self-development. Only 59% of leaders surveyed believed their superiors expected them to participate in self-development (down from 64% in 2010). Among the leaders who thought their superiors supported self-development, only 35% agreed that the chain of command provides the requisite time to accomplish self-development.[83]

Given these statistics, the profession is left with two options. The first option would be establishing an "accountable and reportable" self-development program to reverse this downward trend. Accountability will increase dialogue and awareness to better focus self-development efforts, and reporting these efforts would offer opportunities to identify sources of tacit knowledge among the force that could be applied to yet unknown challenges. The second option is to remind officers of their sworn commitment upon commissioning as captured in Brigadier General S.L.A. Marshall's first edition of the *Armed Forces Officer*. This commitment both inspires and reminds, "the commissioned person must constantly and relentlessly acquire and reacquire the justifications of officership in order to be worthy of the title of officer."[84] Marshall specified that this depended on an officer's willingness to acquire knowledge and internalize duty and service.

Recommendation #3: Introduce Mindfulness-Based Mind Fitness training (MMFT) into institutional leader development programs as a critical skills-based approach necessary to augment existing U.S. Army resilience programs.

In his testimony to Congress on April 9, 2008, then Chief of Staff of the U.S. Army General George Casey testified, "the Army is not broken…it's out of balance."[85]

34

This quote summarized his assessment of the effects of repeated deployments combined with rising statistics of desertion, suicide, and spousal abuse. Now in 2013, even though the Army ceased combat operations in Iraq and is downsizing forces in Afghanistan, eleven years of war continue to take a toll on the force with a growing trend in suicides, mental health concerns, family issues, etc. Without concerted attention, these issues may limit some remarkably talented tactical-level leaders from achieving their full potential as future strategic leaders. The previously mentioned statistics of depression and PTSD include a population of Army leaders potentially susceptible to episodic recurrence of symptoms in the future based on stressful events in the past. Among the thirty-four colonels and below interviewed for this paper, all but one believed methods to improve resilience should be discussed in conjunction with leader development efforts.[86]

The Army's senior leaders recognize the importance of resilience training in responding to organizational uncertainty. Resilience refers to "overall physical and psychological health, and has been described as the ability to 'bounce back from adversity'."[87] Resilience is essential to counter the negative effects of stress and fatigue that contribute to organizational uncertainty. Individuals build resilience from a number of developmental, cognitive, and psychological processes,[88] and more importantly, resilience can be taught and learned.[89]

The Secretary of the Army, John McHugh, recently directed implementation of a "Ready and Resilient" campaign because of his concern that the "abundance of programs" designed to help soldiers contribute to "confusion," lack responsive intervention and are inconsistent in diagnosing PTSD.[90] In addition, he directed the

35

Army to assess the effectiveness of existing programs, including Comprehensive Soldier Fitness (CSF) and the U.S. Army Medical Department's "Resilience Training" (formerly known as "Battlemind Training").[91]

Recent advances in neuroscience provide broader opportunities to address injuries and illnesses affecting the brain, ultimately improving resilience. The opportunities emerging from neuroscience research are not limited to the medical field but also offer practical applications for improving individual resilience. The introduction of "mind fitness," resulting from increased understanding of neuroplasticity, parallels benefits of physical fitness and offers additional possibilities for improvement within the self-development domain.

The theory of neuroplasticity suggests the human brain undergoes structural and functional adaptations in response to repeated experience.[92] These neuroplastic effects can occur from both repeated beneficial experiences, like mind fitness training, or repeated negative experiences. For example, recent studies examining brain regions among persons diagnosed with PTSD showed structural differences in the hippocampus, which is responsible for declarative memory and working memory capacity.[93] Specifically, the PTSD subjects showed smaller hippocampus regions compared to trauma-exposed and non-exposed control groups without PTSD. These hippocampus deficiencies were linked to degraded memory function, which is important to effective leadership from the tactical to strategic level. A previous study among Vietnam War veterans diagnosed with PTSD revealed both a similar structural decrease in hippocampal volume and reduced working memory capacity.[94]

Prolonged stress causes negative neuroplasticity effects that often persist even after the source of stress is no longer present. For example, one study conducted in 2006 showed that returning veterans with service in Iraq demonstrated memory and attention issues more than two months after returning home.[95] This study showed improved reaction time with decreased memory, reduced attention, and lower verbal skills.[96] A subsequent study with the same troops showed decreased attention and memory function immediately following a deployment was correlated with increased PTSD symptoms a year later.[97] Retired General Peter Chiarelli, during his tenure as the Vice Chief of Staff of the Army, reiterated, "For over a decade, nearly every leader and Soldier serving in our Army has lived in a near constant state of anticipation – whether anticipating an upcoming deployment, anticipating the next mission or convoy, or anticipating the challenges of returning home. The prolonged stress and strain on them and their families must be effectively addressed."[98] This prolonged stress that Chiarelli described may be degrading working memory capacity, limiting the ability to regulate existing stress, and reducing tolerance for functioning effectively during additional stress.

However, there are also positive benefits to neuroplasticity. For example, over 30 years of empirical scientific research has documented the positive benefits of neuroplasticity through mindfulness training. Mindfulness is often defined as "bringing one's complete attention to the experiences occurring in the present moment, in a nonjudgmental or accepting way."[99] Mindfulness is noticing what is happening while it is happening; the opposite of mindfulness is being on autopilot. While all humans have the innate ability to be mindful, most live most of the time in an autopilot default mode.[100]

Army leadership literature recognizes "self-awareness" and "emotional intelligence" as components to leadership, and mindfulness clearly offers active possibilities to improve both of these attributes. Mindfulness training offers techniques to cultivate a "mindful" default mode, and mindfulness can lead to positive benefits of neuroplasticity by reducing symptoms of stress, and increasing awareness and insight.[101]

Stress reduction practices through mindfulness are not new. The University of Massachusetts' Center for Mindfulness founded its Mindfulness-Based Stress Reduction Program (MBSR) in 1979 to respond to stress, pain, and illness. Mindfulness-Based Cognitive Therapy (MBCT), created in 1992, has demonstrated success in combining mindfulness and cognitive therapy for "reducing risk of future relapse and recurrence [of depression], presumably through patients acquiring skills, or changes in thinking, that confer some degree of protection against future onsets."[102]

Other applications of mindfulness include Mindfulness-Based Mind Fitness Training (MMFT), which is gaining traction within the U.S. Marine Corps. MMFT focuses on military applications of mindfulness given the inherently stressful, traumatic, and uncertain nature of combat operations that result in negative changes to the brain. The stress associated with decision making in unpredictable environments, treating and managing casualties, and enduring physical and emotional hardships further erode operational effectiveness and "Soldier well being."[103] MMFT is helpful in lessening the harmful effects of these stressful situations.

Dr. Elizabeth Stanley, a former Army officer and professor in Georgetown University's Security Studies Program, conducted extensive research in mind fitness, neuroplasticity and resilience. Her research suggests mind fitness has much in common with physical fitness. Where physical fitness relies on repeated exercises to generate specific muscular and cardiovascular changes, mind fitness similarly relies on specific exercises to create changes in the structure and function of the brain. Where MBSR and MBCT employ principles of neuroplasticity to reduce stress and treat stress-induced illness, MMFT proactively attempts to improve performance by rewiring the brain to be more effective and resilient and thereby decrease the likelihood of stress-induced illness.[104]

MMFT includes three components: Mindfulness skills training to focus attention and build concentration, situational awareness, and non-reactivity; information about stress activation, resilience, and skills to help self-regulation of the autonomic nervous system (which controls the fight-or-flight response); and application of MMFT skills to the operational environment, military missions, and daily routine.[105] MMFT seeks to holistically cultivate personal attributes of attention, mental agility, emotional intelligence, and situational awareness (self, others, and the environment),[106] all foundational capacities necessary for effective leadership. In addition, MMFT improves working memory capacity reversing one of the major correlations with PTSD.[107]

MMFT has also been tested through rigorous neuroscience research beginning with a pilot study evaluating U.S. Marine reservists before and after their deployment to Iraq in 2008. The pilot study demonstrated that Marines who practiced mind fitness exercises outside of the MMFT class, compared to a control group, increased working memory capacity, decreased negative emotions, increased positive emotions, and decreased perceived stress levels.[108] Qualitatively, Marines participating in MMFT testified to new skills in focusing their attention, understanding the stress activation cycle, and learning to better resolve emotions and avoid maladaptive coping behaviors that typically follow deployments. Leaders also noticed improvements in team cohesion and communication.[109] Subsequent larger-scale studies of active Army and Marine units deploying to Afghanistan measured the effectiveness of MMFT through neurocognitive behavioral tasks, blood and saliva bio-markers, heart and respiration rate, self-reporting, and evaluations of performance during actual training events. In addition, a subset of Marines also participated in functional magnetic resonance imaging (fMRI) to record brain activation changes prior to and following both the MMFT class and the deployment. This data from these studies is currently being analyzed, but preliminary results from the 2011 U.S. Marine Corps study were so positive that the Marine Corps is currently testing MMFT embedded into one of its courses at the U.S. Marine Corps School of Infantry.[110]

The U.S. Army's Comprehensive Soldier Fitness (CSF) Program currently serves as the means to increase the baseline resilience of Soldiers. Similar to MMFT, CSF seeks to put "mind or mental fitness on par with physical fitness in terms of training, conditioning, and leader involvement;" however, CSF does not include any skills training to accomplish this objective. Another fundamental difference between MMFT and CSF rests with CSF's reliance on a web-based survey, the Global Assessment Tool (GAT), to measure an individual's resilience in emotional, family, social, and spiritual terms.[111] However, according to Dr. Roy Eidelson and Dr. Stephen Soldz of the Coalition for Ethical Psychology, "the GAT does not include any validated measures that assess PTSD, depression, suicidality, or other major psychological disorders, even though preventing these disorders is a key goal of the CSF program and even though such measures are readily available."[112] Eidelson and Soldz also argue, "There is little evidence that improvement over time in soldiers' GAT scores produces any reduction in the incidence or likelihood of significant psychological distress or other important behavioral health outcomes."[113] More importantly, the CSF Program lacked the pilot testing and rigorous scientific evaluation necessary to determine the effectiveness of the program prior to implementation.[114] Lastly, as individuals receive feedback from the GAT, it is ultimately up to them to "develop goals and a plan to reach those goals."[115] This lack of accountability on the part of the soldier, combined with lack of empirical evidence conclusively validating CSF, potentially only increases the risk to the Army.

Thus, CSF alone may be insufficient for building resilience in the Army, given the steady increase in suicides in spite of the program's implementation in 2008.[116] Secretary McHugh recently reinforced this prospect, "Interventions are not coming as soon as I would like to see them."[117] A complementary approach of combining CSF's "positive psychology" with MMFT's "positive neuroplasticity" methodology may increase resiliency. MMFT also supports the Army's "Ready and Resilient"[118] campaign in offering skills training to increase mental agility, attention, and emotional intelligence skills, thereby increasing resilience and operational readiness. Ultimately, a resilient leader is a more effective leader.

IV. Conclusion

The blending of training, experience, and education occurring over the course of an officer's career remains essential to developing leaders responsive to strategic uncertainty after operations in Iraq and Afghanistan cease. In the context of uncertainty, even simple steps improve the ability to respond effectively. The recommendations offered in this study require minimal investment, in that they do not require or encourage comprehensive reform of proven methods to develop leaders.

Skeptics of accountability in the self-development domain may offer operational tempo and lack of available time for self-development as the primary obstacles to this initiative. While these factors complicate the situation, improved time management can enable opportunities within all three domains of leader development. Further, while the CASAL survey reflected less time afforded to participate in self-development, the majority of Army leaders surveyed (78%) also view self-development as effective to their career progression. Serving in a profession during an era of uncertainty necessitates possession of "expert knowledge" to respond to unknown threats. The Army profession remains accountable to the Nation to accrue such expert knowledge and thus needs to allocate time accordingly. Dedicated self-study provides more opportunities to combine explicit knowledge with tacit knowledge, thereby improving the practical intelligence of the organization as a whole. Pursuit of personal knowledge contributes to the profession, and leaders simply must dedicate time to self-development.

Others might complain that the lack of tangible incentives, in terms of increased promotion or assignment opportunities, related to self-development efforts offer little motivation to pursue personal self-development. A response to this concern is the

emerging "Green Pages" initiative sponsored by the U.S. Army's Office of Economic

Manpower Analysis (OEMA). Headquartered at the United States Military Academy,

"Green Pages" constitutes a database of skills, knowledge, and behaviors to better

"manage talent" within the Army's "Human Capital Model."[119] Officers who disclose self-

development efforts to the "Green Pages" database allow senior leaders, branch

managers, and personnel officers to identify individual officer talents and interests, not

available in traditional personnel systems, that might be appropriate for specific

assignments.

Mindfulness inherently attracts skepticism in the context of Army culture;

however, it is a concept accepted in the medical profession to treat the same issues

present today in the ranks of the U.S Army. Mindfulness also draws upon more than

thirty years of empirical peer-reviewed scientific research. Importantly, the Army

institutionalized "Battlemind" and CSF, programs that lack a similar evidence base. Yet,

these existing Army initiatives face similar degrees of skepticism among both clinical

experts and among soldiers in the force. One critical cause of skepticism for

"Battlemind" and CSF may be that they do not offer methods to regulate stress and

improve mental agility with tools that enhance mission performance as well as increase

resilience as mind fitness does. Mind fitness practices are also consistent with the self-

development domain of Army leader development by increasing cultural savvy

emotional intelligence. Lastly, as the Army addresses issues of resilience and fatigue,

MMFT may provide a credible option to resolve this complicated source of

organizational uncertainty. Practical application of MMFT techniques, already occurring within the U.S. Marine Corps, provides additional opportunities to evaluate the effectiveness of the program.

The good news is that today's Army possesses an incredible depth of knowledge stemming from experience across a wide range of scenarios, which provides a strong foundation to respond to strategic uncertainty. Critical thinking and problem solving are not new to the U.S. Army. The Army's most senior general officers understood the environment associated with the end of the previous "Long War" in Vietnam and engineered an Army that demonstrated overwhelming victory in Operation Desert Storm. Field grade and general officers are well versed in crisis-response, stability, peacekeeping, and security cooperation activities resulting from operations in Grenada, Panama, Somalia, Bosnia, and Kosovo. Following operations in Iraq and Afghanistan, the entire Army contains a large number of soldiers with more than a decade of experience in counterinsurgency, counter-terrorism, humanitarian assistance, and irregular warfare.

Encouraging "bi-lateral" mentorship will offer opportunities to share personal experience across the range of "decisive action" from the tactical to strategic levels. Accountability in personal self-development among a force that already possesses a wide range of contextual understanding across the conflict spectrum will maximize the strength inherent in the Army profession. Lastly, capitalizing on new understanding of neuroscience and employing practical applications of "mind fitness" may offset harmful and detrimental factors that otherwise limit the effectiveness of leaders. Encouraging these efforts will increase the intellectual capacity of the U.S. Army and develop leaders better prepared for a dynamic and uncertain strategic future.

Endnotes

[1] Martin E. Dempsey, "Building Critical Thinkers: Leader Development Must Be Our Top Priority," *Armed Forces Journal*, February 2011, linked at *Armed Forces Journal Homepage*, http://www.armedforcesjournal.com/2011/02/5663450 (accessed December 11, 2012).

[2] Leon Panetta, *Sustaining U.S. Global Leadership: Priorities for 21st Century Defense* (Washington, DC: U.S. Department of Defense, January 2012), 2.

[3] U.S. Department of the Army, *2012 Army Strategic Planning Guidance* (Washington, DC: U.S. Department of the Army, 19 April 2012), 1.

[4] Robert B. Duncan, "Characteristics of Organizational Environments and Perceived Environmental Uncertainty," *Administrative Science Quarterly*, Vol. 17, No. 3 (Sep 1972): 315.

[5] Ibid, 325.

[6] U.S. Congress, Senate, Committee on Armed Services, The Progress in Preventing Military Suicides and Challenges in Detection and Care of the Invisible Wounds of War: Hearing before the Committee on Armed Services, 111th Cong., 2nd sess., June 22, 2010, 1

[7] General Martin E. Dempsey, "Leader Development," *Army*, February 2011, 25.

[8] Robert Kagan and William Kristol, "The Present Danger", *The National Interest*, no. 59 (Spring 2000): 59.

[9] Derek S. Reveron and Kathleen Mahoney-Morris, *Human Security in a Borderless World* (Philadelphia, PA: Westview Press, 2011), 5.

[10] Dan Caldwell and Robert E. Williams, *Seeking Security in an Insecure World* (Lanham, Maryland: Rowman & Littlefield Publishers, 2006), 7.

[11] Mathew Burroughs, "Global Trends 2030," lecture, Georgetown University, Washington, D.C., 24 January 2013.

[12] Office of the Director of National Intelligence, *Global Trends 2030: Alternative Worlds*, ii, http://www.dni.gov/nic/globaltrends (accessed December 12, 2012)

[13] Ibid.

[14] *Global Trends 2030*, iii.

[15] The commonly referred to concept of the "Black Swan" is introduced by Nassim Nicholas Taleb, *The Black Swan: The Impact of the Highly Improbable* (New York: Random House, 2007).

[16] *Global Trends 2030*, iv.

[17] Ibid, ii-xiv.

[18] U.S. Department of the Army, *The U.S. Army Capstone Concept* (Ft. Eustis, VA: U.S. Army Training and Doctrine Command, 19 December 2012), 9.

[19] Robert M. Cassidy, "Back to the Street Without Joy: Counterinsurgency Lessons from Vietnam and Other Small Wars," *Parameters* 34, no. 2 (Summer 2004): 73.

[20] *The U.S. Army Capstone Concept*, 10.

[21] Ivan Shidlovsky, "The World We Live In," briefing slides accompanying 2012 Army Vision Brief, Headquarters, Department of the Army, Washington, D.C., 23 January 2013

[22] Comments from Lieutenant General (Retired) James Dubik, February 15, 2013.

[23] Charles E. Heller and William Stoft, *America's First Battles: 1776-1965* (Lawrence, KS: University Press of Kansas, 1986), ix.

[24] U.S. Department of the Army, *Army 2020: Generating Health & Discipline in the Force Ahead of the Strategic Reset* (Washington DC: U.S. Department of the Army, 2012), 11.

[25] Leonard Wong, et al, "Strategic Leadership Competencies," September 1, 2003, linked from *The Strategic Studies Institute Home Page* at http://www.strategicstudiesinstitute.army.mil/pubs/display.cfm?pubID=382 (accessed on December 15, 2012).

[26] Ibid, 5-6.

[27] Ibid, 6.

[28] Ibid, 7.

[29] Ibid, 8.

[30] Ibid, 9.

[31] Ibid, 9-10.

[32] Ibid.

[33] Interview with Brigadier General Theodore Martin, Commandant of Cadets, United States Military Academy, West Point, New York, November 19, 2012. Thirty-four of forty officers interviewed between October 22, 2012 and January 13, 2013 also agreed with this perception of three generations of officers.

[34] Leonard Wong, "Generations Apart: Xers and Boomers in the Officer Corps," October 1, 2000, linked from the *Strategic Studies Institute Home Page* at http://www.strategicstudiesinstitute.army.mil/pubs/display.cfm?pubID=281 (accessed November 23, 2012).

[35] Ibid, 6.

[36] Ibid, 25.

[37] Walter F. Ulmer, et al, *Leadership Lessons at the Division Command Level – 2010* (Carlisle Barracks, PA: U.S. Army War College, 12 September 2010), 9.

[38] Ibid.

[39] Ibid.

[40] Summary of trends from interviews with officers during the period of October 22, 2012 and January 5, 2013.

[41] Ibid.

[42] Ibid.

[43] Ibid.

[44] U.S. Department of the Army, *Training Units and Developing Leaders,* Army Doctrine Reference Publication 7-0 (Washington DC: U.S. Department of the Army, 23 August 2012), 1-2.

[45] Ibid.

[46] U.S. Department of the Army, *Army Handbook for Self-Development* (Ft. Leavenworth, KS: Center for Army Leadership, 2008), 3

[47] Assessment from interviews with officers ranging from captain to colonel conducted between October 22, 2012 and January 13, 2013 and supported by the main findings of the 2011 Center for Army Leadership Annual Survey of Army Leadership (CASAL), 59-60.

[48] U.S. Army Public Affairs, "Army Announces Optimization of Intermediate Level Education," September 24, 2012, linked from *The United States Army Homepage,* http://www.army.mil/article/87406 (accessed January 9, 2012).

[49] Charles A. Flynn and Wayne W. Grigsby, "The Mission Command Center of Excellence: Driving Institutional Adaptability," *Army*, February 2012, 38.

[50] Brandon Friedman, "Military Suicides Top Combat Deaths – But Only Because the Wars Are Ending," *Time*, January 16, 2013, http://nation.time.com/2013/01/16/military-suicides-top-combat-deaths-but-only-because-the-wars-are-ending/ (accessed January 23, 2013)

[51] *Army 2020: Generating Health & Discipline in the Force*, 22.

[52] Ibid, 28.

[53] Ibid, 45.

[54] Vincent Capaldi, et al, "Sleep disruptions among returning combat veterans from Iraq and Afghanistan," *Military Medicine,* 176, no. 8 (May 2011): 879-88.

[55] *Army 2020: Generating Health & Discipline in the Force*, 22.

[56] Ibid.

[57] Richard Dixon, "PTSD Type Symptoms and CGSC Class 08-01, A Study of Field Grade Officers and Implications for the Future," *Masters of Military Art and Science Monograph* (Ft. Leavenworth, KS: Command and General Staff College, June 13, 2008), ii.

[58] Ibid, 12.

[59] *Army 2020: Generating Health & Discipline in the Force*, 2.

[60] U.S. Army Public Affairs, " CSA Remarks at World Affairs Council of Northern California (As Delivered)," August 24, 2012, linked from *The United States Army Homepage,* http://www.army.mil/article/86263/August_24__2012____CSA_Remarks_at_World_Affairs_Council_of_Northern_California__As_Delivered_/ (accessed August 28, 2012).

[61] Wong, et al., "Strategic Leadership Competencies," 1.

[62] Don M. Snider, "Once Again, the Challenge to the U.S. Army During a Defense Reduction: To Remain a Military Profession," linked at Strategic Studies Institute Homepage at http://www.strategicstudiesinstitute.army.mil/pubs/display.cfm?pubID=1097 (accessed November 19, 2012)

[63] Interview with Lieutenant General David Huntoon, Superintendent, United States Military Academy, West Point, New York, November 19, 2012.

[64] Interview with General Robert Cone, Commanding General, Training and Doctrine Command, Pentagon, Washington, D.C., December 13, 2012.

[65] Kelly Jo Bridgwater, "Decisive Action Training Environment: Future Training Grounded in Today's Intelligence," November 27, 2012, linked from the *U.S. Army Homepage*, http://www.army.mil/article/91690/Decisive_Action_Training_Environment__Future_training_grounded_in_today_s_intelligence/ (accessed January 15, 2013).

[66] Donald Vandergriff, "When Do We Teach the Basics?" *Joint Forces Quarterly*, Issue 58 (3rd Quarter 2010): 71.

[67] This concept of "personal knowledge" presumes explicit knowledge is always grounded in tacit knowledge and is introduced by Michael Polanyi, *Personal Knowledge: Towards a Post-Critical Philosophy* (Chicago, IL: University of Chicago Press, 1958), viii.

[68] Ikujiro Nonaka and Georg von Krogh, "Tacit Knowledge and Knowledge Conversion: Controversy and Advancement in Organizational Knowledge Creation Theory," *Organization Science*, 20, no. 3 (May-June 2009): 638.

[69] Elizabeth Stanley, "Neuroplasticity, Mind Fitness, and Military Effectiveness," *Bio-Inspired Innovation and National Security* (Washington, D.C.: National Defense University Press, 2010), 265.

[70] U.S. Department of the Army, *Army Mentorship Handbook* (Rosslyn, VA: Headquarters, Department of the Army, DCS, G-1, 2005), 6

[71] Stanley McChrystal, "Listen, learn...then lead," March 2011, *Ted* streaming video, 10:10, http://www.ted.com/talks/stanley_mcchrystal.html (accessed December 17, 2012)

[72] Leslie Kwoh, "Reverse Mentoring Cracks Workplace: Top Managers Get Advice on Social Media, Workplace Issues from Young Workers," *The Wall Street Journal*, November 28, 2011, linked from *The Wall Street Journal homepage*, http://online.wsj.com/article/SB10001424052970203764804577060051461094004.html, (accessed on January 5, 2013).

[73] Center for Army Leadership, Technical Report 2012-1, CAL Annual Survey of Army Leadership (CASAL): Main Findings (Fort Leavenworth, KS: Center for Army Leadership, May 2012): 59-60.

[74] Jennifer Hedlund et al, "Tacit Knowledge in Military Leadership: Some Research Products and Their Applications to Leadership Development," Technical Report 1081, United States Army Research Institute for the Behavioral and Social Sciences, May 1998, 3.

[75] Jennifer Hedlund et al, "Identifying and Assessing Tacit Knowledge: Understanding the Practical Intelligence of Military Leaders," *The Leadership Quarterly* 14, no. 2 (April 2003): 117.

[76] Ibid, 118.

[77] Ibid,, 134-137.

[78] Ibid, 133.

[79] Ibid, 118.

[80] Warren Bennis et al, *The Future of Leadership: Today's Top Thinkers Speak to Tomorrow's Leaders* (San Francisco: Josey-Bass, 2001), 98.

[81] U.S. Department of the Army, *Training Units and Developing Leaders,* Army Doctrine Publication 7-0 (Washington DC: U.S. Department of the Army, August 2012), 2

[82] Fallesen, 59.

[83] Ibid, 60.

[84] Reed R. Bonadonna, "Reconsidering the *Armed Forces Officer* of 1950: Democracy, Dialogue, the Humanities, and the Military Profession," *Joint Forces Quarterly*, Issue 68 (1st Quarter 2013): 64.

[85] Tom Bowman, "Army Chief of Staff Casey Defends Iraq Decisions,' January 15, 2009, linked from *National Public Radio homepage*, http://www.npr.org/templates/story/story.php?storyId=99397348, (accessed January 13, 2013)

[86] Interviews with officers ranging from captain to colonel conducted between October 22, 2012 and January 13, 2013.

[87] Paul Lester et al, *The Comprehensive Soldier Fitness Program Evaluation Report #3: Longitudinal Analysis of the Impact of Master Resilience Training on Self-Reported Resilience and Psychological Health Data*, (Washington DC: U.S. Department of the Army, December 2011), 5.

[88] Ibid.

[89] Ibid, 8.

[90] Gary Sheftick, "SECARMY orders 'Ready and Resilient Campaign'," February 5, 2013, linked from the *U.S. Army Homepage*, http://www.army.mil/article/95793/SecArmy_orders__Ready_and_Resilient_Campaign_/ (accessed February 8, 2013)

[91] U.S. Secretary of the Army John McHugh, "Army Ready and Resilient Campaign," memorandum for the Under Secretary and Vice Chief of Staff, U.S. Army, Washington, D.C., February 5, 2013.

[92] Stanley, "Neuroplasticity, Mind Fitness, and Military Effectiveness," 259.

[93] Anke Karl et al, "A meta-analysis of structural brain abnormalities," *Neuroscience and Biobehavioral Reviews* 30 (2006): 1004, linked from http://p113367.typo3server.info/uploads/media/lit0609.pdf (accessed on January 20, 2013)

[94] J. Douglas Bremner, "Hypotheses and Controversies Related to Effects of Stress on the Hippocampus: An Argument for Stress-Induced Damage to the Hippocampus in Patients with Posttraumatic Stress Disorder," *Hippocampus* 11, no. 2 (2001): 75.

[95] Stanley, "Neuroplasticity, Mind Fitness, and Military Effectiveness," 260.

[96] Jennifer Vasterling, et al, "Neuropsychological Outcomes of Army Personnel Following Deployment to the Iraq War," The Journal of the American Medical Association, Vol. 296, No. 5, August 2, 2006, 526.

[97] Brian Marx, et al, "The Influence of Pre-Deployment Neurocognitive Functioning on Post-Deployment PTSD Symptom Outcomes Among Iraq-deployed Army Soldiers," *Journal of the International Neuropsychological Society*, Number 15, 2009, 846.

[98] *Army 2020: Generating Health & Discipline in the Force,* 4.

[99] Ruth A. Baer, et al., "Using Self-Report Assessment Methods to Explore Facets of Mindfulness, *Assessment* 13, no. 1 (March 2006): 27.

[100] Elizabeth Stanley, "Mindfulness-based Mind Fitness Training (MMFT): An Approach for Enhancing Performance and Building Resilience in High Stress Contexts," *The Wiley-Blackwell Handbook of Mindfulness* (Malden, MA: Blackwell Publishing, forthcoming) 13.

[101] Ibid.

[102] John D. Teasdale, et al, "Prevention or Relapse/Recurrence in Major Depression by Mindfulness-Based Cognitive Therapy," *Journal of Consulting and Clinical Psychology*,68, no. 4 (2000): 615-616.

[103] Stanley, "Neuroplasticity, Mind Fitness, and Military Effectiveness," 261.

[104] Ibid, 262.

[105] Elizabeth Stanley and Amishi P. Jha, "Mind Fitness: Improving Operational Effectiveness and Building Warrior Resilience," *Joint Forces Quarterly*, Issue 55 (4th Quarter, 2009): 148.

[106] Stanley, "Neuroplasticity, Mind Fitness, and Military Effectiveness," 267.

[107] Elizabeth Stanley and Amishi P. Jha, "Mind Fitness: Improving Operational Effectiveness and Building Warrior Resilience," 148.

[108] Amishi Jha, Elizabeth Stanley, et al, "Examining the Protective Effects of Mindfulness Training on Working Memory Capacity and Affective Experience," *Emotion* 10, no. 1 (2010): 61.

[109] Elizabeth Stanley, et al, "Mindfulness-based Mind Fitness Training: A Case Study of a High-Stress Predeployment Military Cohort," *Cognitive and Behavioral Practice* 18, no. 4 (November 2011): 573.

[110] Elizabeth Stanley, "Mindfulness-based Mind Fitness Training (MMFT): An Approach for Enhancing Performance and Building Resilience in High Stress Contexts," 21-23.

[111] The Global Assessment Tool (GAT) evaluates the components of physiological/health fitness to allow individuals to develop goals and associated plans to improve these components. See *Army 2020: Generating Health & Discipline in the Force Ahead of the Strategic Reset,* 78.

[112] Roy Eidelson and Stephen Soldz, "Does Comprehensive Soldier Fitness Work? CSF Research Fails the Test," Coalition for an Ethical Psychology Working Paper Number 1, May 2012, 5.

[113] Ibid, 6.

[114] Roy Eidelson, et al, "The Dark Side of Soldier Fitness," *American Psychologist* 66, no. 7 (October 2011): 643.

[115] *Army 2020: Generating Health & Discipline in the Force,* 78.

[116] American Foundation for Suicide Prevention Statistics, "Military Personnel and Veteran Suicide Prevention," linked at http://www.afsp.org/files/Misc_/Public_Policy/ Issue_Briefs/ Mil_Vet_SP_2012_w_bill_info.pdf, (accessed January 25, 2013)

[117] Associated Press, "Army Secretary Visits Joint Base Lewis-McChord to Review Behavioral Health Evaluations," *Washington Post*, February 4, 2013.

[118] U.S. Department of the Army, *Army Strategic Planning Guidance, 2013,* (Washington DC: U.S. Department of the Army, January 2013), 16.

[119] Interview with Major Bill Skimmyhorn and Major John Childress, OEMA, United States Military Academy, West Point, New York, November 19, 2012.